CLASSIC & VINT

TRACTORS

Picture Book

ROBOOKS
PUBLISHING

DIESEL
Standard

JOHN DEERE
620

BELARUS 82

McCORMICK
FARMALL
M

C 19
Sossusvlei
Fordson

Zetor 50 Super

EICHER
Tiger
FR T 2001

J. Oster
Weine - Liköre
COC

MASSEY-HARRIS
744 PD

MASSEY · FERGUSON 65-X

275
MASSEY-FERGUSON

FORD

1630
JOHN DEER

KL I
DIESEL

Printed in Great Britain
by Amazon

29453899R00025